Contents

Opening up the world

Many centuries ago, people in Europe knew next to nothing about the lands of the Far East. The merchants who travelled and traded in the ports round the Mediterranean Sea heard mysterious rumours of fabulous, far-away places that were the source of the precious goods that they sold in Europe. They knew about, and some had even visited, parts of Arabia and India, but the lands beyond remained a mystery.

A modern painting of 10th-century Viking ships. From the 8th to 11th centuries, Viking merchants traded in places as far away as Constantinople (present-day Istanbul).

The main reason for this lack of knowledge was that the Far East was so far away. Today we can fly from one side of the world to the other in a day. But hundreds of years ago, the same journey could take years and was hugely difficult and dangerous. Travellers were stepping into the unknown – literally into unmapped areas – and were at the mercy of treacherous landscapes, stormy seas, bitter cold or searing heat, pirates and **bandits**.

Then, about 700 years ago, all this changed. At that time a book appeared in Europe that gave a detailed, first-hand account of China and many of the lands that lay between Europe and the Far East. It was the record of a **merchant** called Marco Polo who had travelled overland to China, where he remained for more than 20 years.

This book, called *The Travels of Marco Polo*, contained a wealth of information about an unknown world and its peoples. Europeans were amazed when they read his stories about the dazzling court of the **Great Khan**, of strange animals such as crocodiles and giraffes, and of magnificent palaces. Most of the quotations in this book have been taken from a translation of Marco Polo's story.

Marco Polo was born in Venice in what is now Italy, in 1254. He was one of the greatest travellers there has ever been, and many of the sights he saw were not seen again by Europeans for another 500 years. His account of his travels changed the history of the world, for it set in motion a whole series of journeys of exploration that would eventually open up the world. This is the story of Marco Polo's life and adventures.

In Marco's words:

'Emperors and kings, dukes and marquesses, counts, knights, and townsfolk, and all people who wish to know the various races of men and the peculiarities of the various regions of the world, take this book and have it read to you. Here you will find all the great wonders and curiosities of Greater Armenia and Persia, of the Tartars and of India, and of many other territories.'

(Taken from the introduction to *The Travels of Marco Polo*)

Engraving of a medallion issued to commemorate the life and achievements of Marco Polo. The account of his incredible travels opened the eyes of Europeans to an unknown world.

Marco Polo's world

Marco Polo was born in 1254 in the Italian city of Venice. His father was a rich **merchant** called Niccolo Polo. Soon after the birth of his son, Niccolo left Venice on a long trading journey with his brother Maffeo and was away for many years. While they were away, Marco's mother died and the young boy went to live with his aunt.

A queen among cities

By the time Marco was born, Venice was a beautiful city. Its buildings were constructed on islands around a network of canals that were crossed by hundreds of elegant bridges. The canals served as streets, and the Venetians travelled everywhere on small, brightly-coloured boats. Splendid religious processions and **pageants** took place on holy days throughout the year, in which all the people of Venice took part with singing, feasting and dancing.

Venice was not only one of the most beautiful cities in the world, but also controlled one of the most powerful trading empires the world had ever seen.

Saint Mark's, the main church of Venice. It is full of beautiful treasures.

Throughout the city were the great mansions and warehouses of the merchants. Ships came from far away and unloaded their goods at the docks – gold and ivory from Africa, **incense** from Arabia, jewels and perfumed woods from India, and silks and spices from China and the Far East. Throughout the days and into the night, the city hummed with activity as the merchants struck deals and exchanged their goods, while **artisans** transformed many of the goods into objects fit for kings and princes.

Venice grew into such a rich and powerful city because it acted as the trading centre and point of contact between the West and the East. Merchants from northern Europe also came to trade, and in this way many of the goods from the East travelled to cities such as London, Paris and Cologne.

THE ARSENAL

One of the most important places in Venice was the Arsenal, as it was here that the great merchant and military ships were built. These huge wooden vessels transported and protected the precious cargoes that made Venice so rich.

'As one enters the gate there is a great street on either hand with the sea in the middle, and on one side are windows opening out of the houses of the Arsenal, and the same on the other side ... I do not think there is anything finer in the world.'

(Extract from a report on the Arsenal, written by a Spanish visitor to Venice called Pero Tafur)

The Mongol Empire

At the beginning of the 13th century, about 50 years before Marco Polo was born, the entire world was faced with one of the most terrifying threats to its existence. Huge armies of fierce **nomadic** horsemen called **Tartars** poured out of north-east Asia, from a region known today as Mongolia. They were led by brilliant and ruthless commanders whose one aim was to conquer the world. They conquered much of the ancient Chinese Empire and then southern Russia, **Persia**, parts of the Middle East and Eastern Europe.

Deadly warriors

Within 50 years, the **Mongols** (as the Tartars became known) had built up the largest empire ever seen, stretching from China to Eastern Europe. Cities were destroyed and their inhabitants butchered by these terrifying invaders. When they attacked the city of Merv in Central Asia, they are said to have massacred its population of 700,000 citizens, and even killed all the cats and dogs. But although they destroyed many cities in their conquests, the Mongols also brought law and order to their vast empire.

An illustration from a Persian book, showing Genghis Khan and his sons attacking a city. The Mongols struck terror into the hearts of everyone and destroyed many cities.

The first great warrior leader of the Mongols – or **Great Khan** – was Genghis. When he died in 1227, his territories were divided amongst his four sons. One of them, called Ogadai, succeeded him as Great Khan of the Mongol Empire. By 1260, when Marco was six years old, the empire was at its largest extent and was ruled by Kublai, greatest of all the Mongol Great Khans.

Kublai Khan

Kublai Khan (who ruled from 1260 to 1294) was a grandson of Genghis. Upon the death of his brother Mangu, Kublai was elected Great Khan and began one of the most remarkable reigns in history. His reign was a model of wisdom and tolerance. Kublai was keen to learn about the way people outside his empire lived, especially those in the West.

Many Mongols today are skilled horsemen and continue to live their traditional nomadic lives, moving from place to place with their felt yurts (tents). This picture is of a Tuvinian man on horseback, taken in the region of Tuva, to the north of present-day Mongolia.

A NOMADIC PEOPLE

In their native Mongolia, the Tartars had been nomadic **herdsmen**, following their cattle and horses from winter pastures in the plains to summer pastures in the valleys. As they were always on the move, they lived in circular tents made of **felt** that could be packed up and carried on carts. In battle, the Tartars were brilliant horsemen, swooping down on their enemy and firing arrows at lightning speed.

Trade across the world

YOU CAN FOLLOW THE SILK ROAD AND THE SPICE ROUTE ON THE MAP ON PAGES 42–3.

For more than a thousand years before the birth of Marco Polo, valuable goods were traded between East and West. They reached European ports such as Venice by two different routes. The ancient trade route now known as the 'Silk Road' ran overland for 8000 kilometres (5000 miles), from the city of Changan (modern Xi'an) in China. It made its way north-west along the Great Wall of China, across the Taklamakan Desert and up into the Pamir Mountains. The road then continued through Afghanistan and **Persia** and on to the shores of the Mediterranean Sea. Goods were then transferred to ships bound for Europe.

The 'Spice Route' travelled about 15,000 kilometres (9000 miles) across the sea, from ports in China and the Spice Islands (the Maluku Islands in present-day Indonesia), across the Indian Ocean and then up the Persian Gulf or the Red Sea and so on to the Mediterranean Sea. From there the goods were transported to Europe.

In a pilgrim's words:

'*There is snow both in winter and in summer, winds, rain, drifting sand and gravel storms. The road is difficult and broken, with steep crags and precipices in the way ... on going forward there is no sure foothold.*'

(Taken from the writings of a 5th-century Chinese pilgrim called Fa Xian, describing the eastern part of the Silk Road)

A 13th-century illustration of an Arabic ship. Arab sailors were very skilled and travelled long distances across the seas.

A camel caravan crossing the desert. Camels were known as the 'ships of the desert' and camel caravans can still be seen in parts of Arabia today.

Goods and knowledge

The convoys of ships and the **caravans** of camels and horses were piled high with the luxuries of the East – not only silks and spices, but also exotic woods, rare animals and plants, jewels and ivory. These were exchanged for western goods such as gold and silver, coral and amber, and cotton and woollen cloth.

However, the Silk Road and Spice Route also acted as paths for the exchange of knowledge – new ideas on technology and science, languages, art and religion. Some of the most important skills, such as writing, weaving, agriculture and riding, and some of the world's great religions, were carried along the trade routes in this way.

A RELAY SYSTEM

Few **merchants** travelled the whole of the trade routes. Instead, they bought goods from merchants in one region, travelled some distance and then sold them on to another group of merchants, in a sort of relay system. The goods were therefore bought and sold several times on their long journey. The merchants at the western end of the trade routes never knew exactly where the eastern goods came from, so many weird and wonderful stories grew up about their origins.

The Polos first go east

As far back as the time of Ancient Greece and Rome, goods from the Far East, India and Arabia had been carried along trade routes to **merchants** in Europe. But as the Roman Empire declined in the 4th and 5th centuries AD, trading became more and more difficult. Gradually, **nomadic** tribes in Central Asia cut off nearly every contact between East and West. Venice remained one of the very few European points of contact with the East.

Brave priests

But the Polos were not the first Europeans to visit the **Mongols** in their distant lands. Following the Mongol conquests of the 13th century, many European countries feared that they would be attacked next. But once it became clear that this was not going to happen, European rulers began to regard the Mongols as possible allies against their long-standing enemies, the Turks. In 1245, **Pope** Innocent IV sent a **Franciscan** priest as **ambassador** to the court of the **Great Khan**. Another Franciscan priest followed him in 1253. Although the Mongols did not want to join these missions against the Turks, they were at least willing to receive ambassadors from the western world.

An **illuminated** letter E from a 13th-century book, showing William of Rubrouk (one of the figures at the bottom). He was a monk sent by the King of France to meet the Great Khan in 1253.

The Polo brothers

In the early 1260s, when Marco was about 6, Niccolo and Maffeo Polo were returning from a trade mission to the Crimea, when they found their return route to Venice blocked by two Mongol armies preparing to fight each other. They were forced to make a long detour to the Central Asian city of Bukhara. There they met a Mongol ambassador who invited them to **Cathay** (China). His master, Kublai Khan, 'had never seen any Latin (European) and very much wanted to see one'.

In Marco's words:

'The Great Khan also gave the brothers and his baron a tablet of gold, on which was written that the three emissaries, wherever they went, should be given all the lodging they might need and horses and men to escort them from one land to another.'

(Taken from the introduction to *The Travels of Marco Polo*)

An illustration of Niccolo and Maffeo Polo first meeting Kublai Khan, from a 15th-century book called Le Livre des Merveilles du Monde.

The two brothers set off for the new Mongol capital of Khanbaliq (now Beijing) which they reached one year later. Kublai Khan was delighted to see them and asked them many questions. He was particularly interested in finding out about the Pope and Christian beliefs. Their visit was a great success, and after two years in China they started back to Venice with a friendly letter from Kublai Khan to the pope. Finally, in 1269, the Polos arrived home in Venice.

A new adventure

When Niccolo and Maffeo Polo finally arrived back home, they heard that the **pope** had died and a new one had not yet been elected. Kublai Khan had given the brothers a letter asking the pope to send 100 of his most learned **scholars** to try to prove to the **Great Khan** that Christianity was the best religion. He also asked the Polos to return with some oil from the lamp that hangs in the Church of the Holy Sepulchre in Jerusalem.

Off to Cathay

After two years of waiting for the election of a new pope, they could delay no longer. They were afraid of losing their contact with the Great Khan. This time they decided to take Niccolo's son Marco with them. He was now 17 and must have been overwhelmed with excitement at the prospect of such a journey.

Weeks of preparation followed until finally, in the summer of 1271, the Polos set sail from Venice, bound for the port of Acre across the Mediterranean (in present-day Israel). This was the start of an adventure that would keep them away for 24 years. They were a small group, just the three Polos themselves and a few servants.

YOU CAN FOLLOW THE POLOS' JOURNEY ON THE MAP ON PAGES 42–3.

An illustration from Le Livre des Merveilles du Monde *showing Niccolo, Maffeo and Marco Polo setting out from Venice on the first leg of their journey to China.*

From Acre they travelled overland on horseback to Jerusalem to collect the oil for Kublai Khan. They set out northwards for the town of Ayas (in present-day Turkey) for the first stage of their journey to join the Silk Road to China. But no sooner had they left than a messenger caught up with them with the news that a new pope, Gregory X, had at last been elected.

The new pope summoned the Polos back to Acre. While he could not send the hundred Christian scholars to the Great Khan, he did send the two most senior priests in the Holy Land. At last they had a real message of goodwill from the pope to take to the Great Khan. They all set off from Acre once again, in high spirits. But their hopes were about to be shattered.

One of the chapels inside the Church of the Holy Sepulchre in Jerusalem, which was built over the place where Jesus was crucified. At the heart of the church is the tomb (Holy Sepulchre) where Jesus was buried. The church seen today was built by the Crusaders and has undergone a long series of disasters and rebuilding. Kublai Khan asked Niccolo and Mafeo Polo to bring him some oil from a lamp in this church.

A change of plan

You can follow the Polos' journey on the map on pages 42–3.

When the Polos arrived in Ayas, they heard the news that the Mamelukes, the rulers of Egypt, were attacking the lands that they were planning to cross. The two priests who had been sent by the **pope** were alarmed by this news, refused to go any further and were escorted back to Acre.

But the Polos carried on regardless. From Ayas they travelled through a region known as Lesser Armenia. Along the way, Marco was drinking in all the sights. The people in this region were Christian but they were subjects of the **Great Khan**, far away in China. Wherever he went, he saw that people were allowed to practise their different religions freely, and he was very impressed by the tolerance of the Mongol government.

A weekly market in Turkey. Marco Polo would have witnessed similar scenes, when country people sold their produce and livestock in the towns and cities.

The Polos moved on into Greater Armenia, between the Caucasus Mountains and upper **Mesopotamia**. They passed Mount Ararat, where Noah's Ark was believed to have landed, and where 'the snow lies so deep all the year round that no one can ever climb it'. They were travelling on horseback at an average of 16 kilometres (10 miles) an hour a day.

In Marco's words:

'They weave the choicest and most beautiful carpets in the world. They also weave silk fabrics of crimson and other colours, of great beauty and richness, and many other kinds of cloth.'

(Marco's description of the Turkomans in The Travels)

16

An illustration from a book called Les Livres du Graunt Caam, *showing the three Magi visiting the newborn Jesus Christ. Marco Polo heard thet the Magi were believed to be buried in the town of Saba.*

Finally the Polos reached the Persian town of Saba, to the south of the Caspian Sea. From there they travelled south to the city of Kerman, famous for its fine work in steel, and then through a bitterly cold mountain pass. Down below they entered a fertile plain where humped oxen (**zebu**) grazed. 'There are also sheep as big as asses, with tails so thick and plump that they weigh a good thirty pounds. Fine, fat beasts they are, and good eating.'

Under attack

Beyond this peaceful plain they entered an area controlled by a bloodthirsty robber tribe called the Caraunas. 'It is a bad and dangerous road, being infested by robbers.' For safety, the Polos joined up with a larger **caravan**, but during a dust storm they were attacked and the caravan scattered. The Polos escaped to a small village, but many other members of the party were killed or captured and later sold into slavery.

They now headed south to the port of Hormuz on the Persian Gulf, where they planned to take a ship to **Cathay**. But when they saw the ships they changed their minds. Marco said that they were badly built and it would have been 'a risky undertaking to sail in these ships'. They decided that it would be safer travelling overland after all, and so they went north again, back to Kerman.

17

The hazards of travel

Early sea travellers and explorers like the Polos were always at the mercy of unfamiliar currents and sudden storms. Once they were out of sight of land they were in danger of getting lost. If they sailed too close to land they could be smashed against rocks. By day they used the sun to plot their course, and by night the stars. But when these were obscured by clouds they had nothing to guide them. Even the shortest journey was filled with danger. Many people lost their lives and every kilometre of coastline and every new island was won at great cost.

Travel by land was just as dangerous. Apart from the hazard of attack by wild animals, **bandits** or hostile armies, travellers by land were also venturing into the unknown. They could carry only a limited amount of supplies and many died from thirst. They had to contend with towering mountains, bitter cold or scorching heat. They could be lashed by driving rain or freezing snow or choked by sand storms.

An illustration from a 16th-century book, showing Arab merchants being attacked by bandits. Rich trade caravans were always at the mercy of bandits.

Growing knowledge

Slowly, people gathered enough information from these early journeys to allow them to draw maps. At first these maps were very simple, and in some cases the information they gave was wrong. But gradually, the more details that travellers brought back, the more the gaps in the maps could be filled, presenting a more and more accurate picture.

In the same way, travellers by land and sea developed instruments to help them judge distances and to work out directions. The accuracy of these instruments could mean life or death to the travellers. The magnetic compass, for example, was used to tell them in which direction they were going. Compasses were used in China from about AD 1050, and in Europe from 1187. The astrolabe was an instrument used by travellers to work out where they were from the position of the sun, moon and stars.

A 9th-century astrolabe. Astrolabes were used by early astronomers to calculate the position of the stars and planets. They were also used as navigational devices.

MONSOONS AND TRADE WINDS

Mariners sailing the Indian Ocean soon worked out that winds could be used to their advantage. For centuries before the time of Marco Polo, Arabian and Indian sailors had travelled between the Indian ports and the Red Sea with the help of regular seasonal winds. These are the monsoon winds that blow from the south-west from April to October, and from the north-east from October to April. Similarly, ships from ports in China could catch the trade winds (so called because they were used by traders) of the China Sea in late autumn.

Across the Roof of the World

From Hormuz, the Polos had to travel 322 kilometres (200 miles) overland back to Kerman. This time they took extra care and sent guards ahead of them to keep a look-out for **bandits**. Eventually they reached Kerman where they rested for a few days before starting out again.

An illustration from Les Livres du Graunt Caam, *showing the Polos entering a town on 'the great river Balacian', which they crossed before their climb into the Pamir Mountains.*

Up into the mountains

Before them lay endless stretches of desert. No trees grew there and any water they saw was green and so bitter that they could not drink it. The swirling wind stung their faces and the hot sand burned their feet. At last they saw the snow-covered peaks of towering mountains in the far distance. These were the mighty Pamirs, known as the 'Roof of the World'.

YOU CAN FOLLOW THE POLOS' JOURNEY ON THE MAP ON PAGES 42–3.

Leaving the desert behind them, the Polos slowly climbed higher and higher into the mountains. But the higher they got, the thinner the air became and the more difficult it was to breathe. When they stopped to camp for the night, Marco noticed that it was impossible to burn a good fire. He thought that this was because of the cold air, but today we know that it was because they were very high up, where there is little oxygen in the air.

Travellers through the Pamir Mountains believed that the ghostly noises of the bitter wind whistling through the rocks were really made by spirits called djinns. They had to be on their guard because these spirits could lead them off the path to their deaths.

After 12 days, the Polos came down the other side into gentle valleys with green fields and lakes. They crossed the northern part of Kashmir, which Marco believed was one of the most beautiful places he had ever seen. Finally they reached the outer fringes of China itself. They could rest here before beginning the next leg of their journey through the Taklamakan Desert, one of the most desolate regions on earth.

In Marco's words:

'Ascending mountain after mountain, you at length arrive at a point where you might suppose the surrounding summits to be the highest lands in the world ... So great is the height of the mountains, that no birds are to be seen near the summits ... Fires when lighted do not give the same heat as in lower situations.'

(Marco Polo's description of his crossing of the Pamirs in 1273)

A view across the Korfornihon Valley in Tajikistan, at the eastern end of the Pamir Mountains. Marco Polo travelled through spectacular landscapes such as this.

The Taklamakan Desert

A Bactrian camel, like the ones the Polos used in the eastern part of their journey. Camels were ideal for carrying heavy loads over long distances in regions where there was little food and water.

The Taklamakan Desert (in north-western China) stretched before them for hundreds of miles to the east. 'This desert is reported to be so long that it would take a year to go from end to end; and at the narrowest point it takes a month to cross it. It consists entirely of mountains and sand and valleys. There is nothing at all to eat.'

Singing sands

They were lucky, for the part of the Silk Road that crossed the desert was well known. There were 20 resting places along the way, but there was little water to be found at any of them and at some it was undrinkable. They saw no animals or birds, but sometimes they passed the bleached bones of some unfortunate traveller and his camel. They had heard terrifying stories of **mirages** and evil spirits that lured travellers to their deaths. They were told that sometimes travellers would hear musical instruments, singing and the cries of battle. Today these sounds can still be heard, in areas called the 'singing sands', and are known to be caused by shifting sand dunes.

YOU CAN FOLLOW THE POLOS' JOURNEY ON THE MAP ON PAGES 42–3.

Lost in the desert

One day Marco himself got lost when he rode away from his party to look at a rock. He turned round and found himself completely alone. He thought he heard his voice being called but it was only the winds mocking him. He had no idea which direction to take and was very relieved when his uncle Maffeo finally found him.

It took the Polos about 30 days to cross the desert, and the first city they came to was Suchow. They were now in an area where **Buddhists** lived, and Marco found their religious customs very strange. Here, only about 40 days' journey from Kublai Khan, they were met by a royal escort and led to his magnificent summer palace at Shangdu. At last in 1274, after a journey of three and a half years, they came face to face with the **Great Khan** himself.

In Marco's words:

'When a man is riding through the desert by night and ... he gets separated from his companions ..., he hears spirit voices talking to him as if they were his companions ... Often these voices lure him away from the path and he never finds it again, and many travellers have got lost and died because of this.'

(Marco's description of the Taklamakan Desert from *The Travels*)

A view of the Taklamakan Desert. This was one of the most dangerous stages of the Polos' journey. They had very little to eat and drink, while mirages and strange sounds made their crossing even more difficult.

At the court of the Great Khan

Niccolo, Maffeo and Marco Polo were led into the presence of Kublai Khan. Marco had been looking forward to this moment ever since he had left Venice. The three weary but excited travellers prostrated themselves on the ground before the ruler of the greatest empire the world had ever seen. Kublai Khan then celebrated their arrival with a splendid **banquet**.

Renewed friendships

Kublai Khan was pleased to see the two brothers again and interested to hear the message they had brought from the **pope**. He was also interested to listen to the story of their journey and all the adventures they had experienced along the way. Niccolo introduced his son Marco to him as 'my son and your servant'. Kublai answered, 'He is welcome and I am very pleased.' Marco was now 21 years old and had grown into an intelligent young man. The long and exciting journey to China had tested his courage, and he had learned many new things at every stage.

Marco was very impressed by the **Great Khan**, who was at this time about 60 years old. He described him as 'neither short nor tall, but of medium height. His arms and legs are well fleshed out and shapely. His complexion is fair and ruddy like a rose, his eyes black and handsome, the nose shapely and set squarely in place.'

*A portrait of Kublai Khan (1216–94). He was the first **Mongol** ruler to call himself Emperor of China.*

Like his **Tartar** ancestors who had led **nomadic** lives in the huge plains of Central Asia, Kublai was always happiest when he was out hunting in the park that surrounded his palace at Shangdu. Marco recorded that when the Great Khan was in the field he would rest in a magnificent tent made of silk and perfumed woods such as sandalwood, decorated inside with cloth woven with gold thread and lion skins. He also said that Kublai owned a stable of more than 10,000 pure white horses.

The Great Wall of China. It was built in the 3rd century BC, about 1500 years before Marco Polo's journey. It stretches for more than 3000 km (2000 miles) across mountains and valleys.

Kublai would spend every June, July and August at his palace at Shangdu. Magicians and healers from Tibet and Kashmir were also housed there. Marco claimed that they used spells to drive away rain clouds so that the skies around the palace were always bright and sunny. He reported that at royal banquets the Tibetan magicians could make cups full of wine and milk fly through the air, so that drinks reached Kublai Khan without being held by human hands.

25

Khanbaliq and the wonders of Cathay

After spending the summer months at Shangdu, Kublai Khan and his Court returned to the capital city of Khanbaliq (which means 'The City of the Great Khan'), modern Beijing. The Polos had been taken into the service of Kublai Khan and so they accompanied the rest of the courtiers and officials.

Marco was amazed by what he saw. The city was huge and bustling with life. The busy streets were wide and straight and filled with the shops and warehouses of merchants and craftsmen. Most of the people he saw were Chinese, but there was a special part of the city where foreign merchants and craftsmen lived and worked. He saw large houses with courtyards and gardens. Strong stone walls encircled the whole city.

A copy of a map made in 1459. It shows China and its main cities, and is based on Marco Polo's descriptions.

At the centre of the city lay Kublai Khan's winter palace, surrounded by a beautiful park. Marco describes it as 'a palace of great size and beauty with many halls and residential quarters'. Wide marble steps led up to the palace, which had a brightly-coloured roof. Inside, the walls and ceilings were decorated with paintings and fancy carvings in gold and silver.

More wonders

Marco was dazzled by the splendour of the Great Khan's palace and by the magnificent **banquets** held there. But he was also amazed by some of the other things he saw for the first time in Khanbaliq. Paper money was one of these. 'To each note a number of officers ... not only subscribe their names but also affix their seals.' Nearly as impressive as paper money was the efficient postal service that criss-crossed China, with its riders who covered 250 miles a day. Another wonder for Marco was 'stones that burn like logs', which were obviously coal. This was unknown as a fuel in Venice at this time.

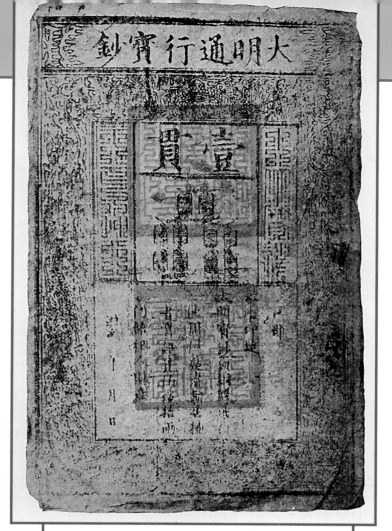

An example of Chinese paper money. This note was made about 100 years after Marco Polo's visit, but is similar to the notes he would have seen.

In Marco's words:

'The roof blazes with scarlet and green and blue and yellow and every colour, so brilliantly varnished that it glitters like crystal and the sparkle of it can be seen far away.'

(Part of Marco's description of the palace at Khanbaliq)

THE EMPEROR'S WIVES

Marco records that Kublai Khan had four wives, by whom he had 22 sons. (Kublai Khan also had many daughters, but Marco did not mention them, probably because they were considered to be less important than the sons.) The wives lived in separate buildings in the palace park. Each was called empress and Marco described how 'each of these ladies has in her court ten thousand persons'.

Missions to Mongol lands

You can follow Marco's travels on the map on pages 42–3.

Niccolo and Maffeo had been the leaders of the expedition from Venice to China. The purpose of their trip was essentially one of trade. But soon after their arrival in Khanbaliq, Marco began to take over as the more important member of the family. Kublai Khan was very impressed by the young man's quick intelligence, his ability to notice interesting and unusual things and his skill at learning languages. The **Great Khan** had been looking for someone with these abilities. As a result, he gave Marco special powers and responsibilities.

The battle between the commanders of the Great Khan and the King of Mien (Burma), from *Le Livre des Merveilles du Monde, printed in the 15th century.*

Ambassador to the Great Khan

Marco was to serve the Great Khan for 17 years, working as a **diplomat** on missions round the Mongol Empire and beyond. 'It happened that Marco ... acquired an impressive knowledge of the customs of the **Tartars**, their **dialects** and their letters ... When Marco went on his mission ... he paid close attention to all the novelties and curiosities that came his way, so that he could describe them to the Great Khan.'

Marco's first mission was to Yunnan province, about four months' journey from Khanbaliq. He also travelled into Tibet and Burma. All along the way he took careful notes on the spectacular scenery he passed through. In Tibet he was impressed by the huge bamboo forests, but he also said that the area was full of 'the greatest rogues and greatest robbers in the world'.

Of the Burmese capital, Pagan, he wrote: 'Once a rich and powerful king lived in this city. His dying command was that two towers, one of gold and one of silver, should be built over his tomb or monument.'

Marco's second mission was to the province of Mangi in south-east China. In this region he saw the mighty Yangtze River, which he said was so wide in places that it looked like the sea. The city of Kinsai (modern Hangchow) was the 'finest and most splendid in the world'.

Each time Marco returned to Khanbaliq from one of his official tours, he would go immediately to the royal palace and report his findings to the emperor. Kublai Khan had great faith in his new servant, mainly because Marco was a foreigner and was able to give very accurate, balanced reports on all he saw. This gave Kublai valuable information on many parts of his empire.

Beyond the empire

As well as being interested in his own territories, Kublai Khan wanted to learn more about the people and places beyond the borders of the **Mongol** Empire. Once again, Marco Polo was the ideal person to send on these voyages of exploration and discovery.

YOU CAN FOLLOW MARCO'S TRAVELS ON THE MAP ON PAGES 42–3.

West to India

Marco sailed from the great Chinese port of Zaiton (now Amoy) in a large ocean-going wooden ship called a **junk**. This was much better made than the ships he had seen in Hormuz. He sailed down the coast of China to the island of Hainan. 'In the year 1285 I, Marco Polo, was in this country and at that time this king [of Hainan] had 326 children ...'

The Sleeping Buddha in a Sri Lankan temple. Marco Polo visited Ceylon (now Sri Lanka), known as 'the island of rubies', while in the service of Kublai Khan.

He sailed on to Java, the centre of the spice trade. 'This is the source of most of the spice that comes into the world's markets.' Then, in Sumatra, he had to wait five months for calm weather. There he saw a rhinoceros for the first time, which he described as a unicorn. He also saw 'men with tails' – probably large monkeys.

Next, they sailed to the Andaman Islands and then Ceylon (now Sri Lanka). Marco's reason for visiting Ceylon was to bring back the holy tooth of the **Buddha**. This was a very famous and holy **relic** revered by all **Buddhists**. It was believed to be a tooth from the jaw of the Buddha himself. Marco succeeded in this, but while in Ceylon he was unable to buy the largest ruby in the world, which was 'the most brilliant object to behold ... glowing red like fire'.

From Ceylon, Marco crossed to India. He saw divers fishing for pearls. 'The place where pearls are most plentiful is called Betala, and is on the mainland.' He travelled around the region in the south-east known today as the Deccan Peninsula. He saw **Hindu** priests in Maarbar and marvelled at the worship of cattle. To the north he went to Motupalli, which was ruled by a wise queen. This was at a time when very few women in Europe held positions of power. 'Never was lady or lord so well beloved as she is by her subjects.' This region was also rich in diamonds.

An illustration from Les Livres du Graunt Caam, *showing pearl-divers. Marco Polo was very impressed by the pearl-divers on the west coast of India and described their activities in great detail in* The Travels: *'For you must know that pearls gathered in this gulf are exported throughout the world, because most of them are round and lustrous.'*

After months of seeing these wonders, Marco sailed back to China, his ship full of treasures and his head full of information for the **Great Khan**.

The journey home

Marco, Maffeo and Niccolo Polo had now been away from their home in Venice for 20 years. For some time they had wanted to return. While Marco was on his diplomatic missions for the **Great Khan**, Niccolo and Maffeo continued their work as **merchants**. They were now old men and had been home only once in 37 years. But Kublai Khan did not want to lose such valuable servants, and each time they raised the subject with him he chose to ignore them.

Finally, in 1292, their opportunity to leave China arrived. By a stroke of luck, **ambassadors** from Arghun, Khan of **Persia**, arrived at Khanbaliq with a request that the Great Khan send one of the royal princesses to Persia to be Arghun's new wife. Kublai chose Princess Cocachin.

Marco at this time had just returned from his trip to India. With his experience of sea travel, the Great Khan's advisers suggested that Marco, and Niccolo and Maffeo, should accompany the princess to Persia by sea. Kublai reluctantly agreed and appointed them his special ambassadors to the **pope** and all the rulers of Europe. He was sad to see them go and both sides knew that they would never see each other again. Kublai was now a very old man and the journey back to Italy would take some years.

An illustration from Les Livres du Graunt Caam, *showing Indian ships docking in the great Chinese port of Zaiton. It was from here that the Polos sailed from China for the last time.*

The party consisted of 2000 people, who left the port of Zaiton in 14 ships in the spring of 1292, bound for India. It took them 21 months to reach Hormuz on the Persian Gulf, and during that time about 580 of their party died from accidents or disease.

The Polos escorted Princess Cocachin inland to Kerman where they said goodbye to her. They then continued their journey home. They finally reached Venice in 1295, 'with many riches, thanking God who had delivered us from so many great labours and infinite perils'.

Their homeward journey had taken three years, and they had been away altogether for 24 years. Just the year before, in 1294, Kublai Khan had died, and with his death the golden age of the Mongol Empire ended.

YOU CAN FOLLOW THE POLOS' JOURNEY ON THE MAP ON PAGES 42–3.

A view of the church of Hagia Sophia in Constantinople (Istanbul) in Turkey. The Polos stopped at the city on their way home.

THE END OF AN ERA

Kublai Khan's empire stretched right across Asia, but it was China that he made his home, with Khanbaliq as his capital. He adopted Chinese manners and called himself the first Chinese emperor of the Yuan dynasty. Kublai Khan was 80 years old when he died in 1294, and the 34 years of his reign were a golden age in Chinese history, when he encouraged the arts and sciences and welcomed foreigners to his splendid court.

Strangers in Venice

As the Polos' ship docked in Venice, all the familiar sites and sounds came back to Marco. There were the houses, narrow alleyways and canals he had got to know as a boy. But he had been away for so long (24 years) that there were also many new buildings and other changes, and it seemed so strange to be back in the city that had become just a distant memory to all of them.

A cool reception

The weary travellers were in for a surprise – they did not receive the warm welcome they were expecting. When the door of their home was opened, their family and servants could not believe that the three untidy-looking men standing on the doorstep were really the travellers returned. Their family had heard no news about them for so long that they had accepted that they would never return. The possessions of the three had been divided up amongst other members of the family, and these people were reluctant to give them back again!

An illustration of the Polos' return to their home in Venice, taken from a book called The Book of Ser Marco Polo, *by Sir Henry Yule, published in 1903.*

> *They had 'an indescribable something of the Tartar in their aspect and in their way of speech, having almost forgotten the Venetian tongue. Their garments were much the worse for wear, made of coarse cloth, and cut after the fashion of the Tartars.'*
>
> (A description of the Polos by a family friend)

What were Marco, his father and uncle to do to convince their family that they really were back? They arranged a **banquet** to which they invited all their relatives. They washed and dressed in some of the magnificent clothes they had brought back from China.

Towards the end of the banquet, the three left the room and changed back into the rough clothes they had first arrived in. They returned to their guests and then ripped open the seams of their clothes. Out poured a brilliant cascade of sparkling jewels – rubies, emeralds, sapphires and diamonds – which they had sewn into their clothes before they left China.

Now their relatives were finally convinced that the long-lost travellers had returned, and they were welcomed back into the heart of the family. But whether they believed any of the fantastic stories that the three told them is a different matter. At a time when there was very little information about the East and certainly no photographs, many of these sounded so astonishing to Europeans that it was difficult for them to believe them.

Precious stones from India and the Far East were highly prized in Europe where they were used to decorate beautiful jewellery like this gold chain.

Marco's marriage and later life

Marco was 39 when he returned to Venice, and he lived for another 31 years. Little is known about his later life, except that he returned to live in the family house and became a **merchant**, like his father. At about the age of 45, he married a rich Venetian woman called Donata Badoer. Little is known about her. They had three daughters and a number of grandchildren, but beyond them no family descendants have been traced.

How we know

The story of Marco Polo's incredible journeys would probably never have been recorded had there not been another twist of fate. Venice and another Italian city, Genoa, had rival trading empires. Sea battles frequently broke out between the two cities. In about 1297, Marco was travelling in a fleet of Venetian ships when they were attacked by the Genoese. Marco, along with hundreds of others, was captured.

Illustration of a Venetian galley at the Battle of Curzola, between Venice and Genoa. It was during this sea battle that Marco Polo was captured.

He was taken to Genoa and thrown into prison. One of his cell-mates was a man called Rustichello of Pisa. To while away the long hours, Marco started to recount some of his stories. Rustichello was fascinated and the two of them decided to set the stories down as a book. As Marco related the amazing tales, Rustichello took detailed notes. After two years, when the war between Genoa and Venice was over, Marco returned home.

Copies of *The Travels of Marco Polo* were written down in Latin and some other Italian **dialects** apart from Venetian. The book immediately became very popular among important people in Venice and was translated into other European languages, including French and English. The first printed copies of the book were produced in 1477. A few copies of these survive today.

Marco died in 1324, aged 70. By then he was not a rich man, and in his will he left all his modest possessions to his three daughters. He also mentioned in his will that his slave and servant Peter, a **Mongol** who had travelled back with him, should be set free.

Some of Marco's stories seemed so incredible that many people thought he must have made them up. As Marco lay dying, the priest bent over him and asked him if he would like to take back at least some of the more fantastic stories that were recorded in his book, so as to clear his conscience with God before he died. Marco is supposed to have said quietly, 'I never told the half of what I saw.'

Marco Polo's will. He left his few possessions to his wife and daughters.

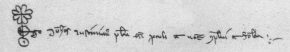

Explorers who followed

Marco Polo, his father and uncle were among the first Europeans to travel to China. A few more Europeans did follow in their footsteps, and some of them wrote about their journeys. In 1320, just four years before Marco's death, an Italian Christian missionary priest called Father Odoric di Pordenone travelled overland to China. It is unknown whether he had ever met Marco Polo, or even read *The Travels*. Odoric later wrote a book about his journey, in which he claimed that 'there are now many people in Venice who have visited Kinsai [modern Hangchow]'.

The Chinese go west

There were, however, other journeys made in the early 15th century – this time from East to West. Between 1405 and 1433, a Chinese admiral called Cheng Ho made seven voyages and visited places such as Indochina, Java, Sumatra and Thailand. He was in command of more than 27,000 men and a fleet of 317 ships. They reached as far as the Persian Gulf and the east coast of Africa.

A traditional Chinese junk in the port of Hong Kong. Cheng Ho's fleet of ships looked like this but they were much bigger.

FRANCISCO PEGOLOTTI

In about 1340, an Italian **merchant** called Francisco Pegolotti wrote a book called *The Merchants' Handbook* which included advice for merchants bound for China. Soon afterwards, China turned its back on the rest of the world and a veil was drawn across the country that would hide it for hundreds of years.

Some of the ships may have reached the northern coast of Australia. Another group may even have rounded the Cape of Good Hope (the southern tip of Africa), because a Chinese map of 1420 clearly shows part of Africa's west coast. This was 60 years before Bartolemeu Diaz became the first European to round the Cape. Two years after Cheng Ho returned from his final expedition, a new foreign policy was adopted and all contact with the West was stopped.

Christopher Columbus

For many centuries in Europe, *The Travels* remained the most detailed record of a remarkable period of contact between West and East. It set in motion a European fascination with the East that would culminate in the great sea voyages of discovery centuries later. Two hundred years after it was first published, *The Travels* inspired Christopher Columbus to sail westwards across the Atlantic on what he believed to be the most direct route to **Cathay**. Instead, he found the West Indies and America.

An illustration of a Chinese emperor and empress, taken from a book published in 1590. By this time China had cut off all contact with the West.

The legacy of Marco Polo

Amongst the treasures and curiosities that Marco Polo brought back from his travels were some **yak** wool, a piece of **asbestos** cloth, the dried head of a **musk deer**, some **sago**, and the seeds of various plants. These had never been seen in Europe before and they were just a tiny sample of the amazing variety of things to be found in the East.

An illustration of Marco Polo as a young man. This is taken from the title page of the first printed edition of his book, dated 1477.

A lasting treasure

The main thing that Marco brought back with him, however, was knowledge – the knowledge of a whole unknown world, with different people and their customs. All this information was set down in his book *The Travels of Marco Polo*, one of the most remarkable and famous books ever written. It is this book, and the knowledge it contains, that is Marco's lasting legacy to the world.

Another important legacy of Marco Polo's life and travels was his record of the **Mongol** Empire at its peak. When Kublai died in 1294, he was succeeded as **Great Khan** by his grandson Temur. Temur died in 1307 and there followed 50 years of fighting between the Mongols and the Chinese. In 1368, the Mongols were driven out of China. From early in the next century the new Chinese Ming emperors forbade any European visitors.

Further west, the Mongol Empire started to break up until the whole overland route between Europe and the Far East was blocked to travellers. This marked the end of relations between East and West for many centuries. Marco's record of his travels was therefore the last detailed European account of that part of the world for more than 500 years.

Ongoing journey

The Travels of Marco Polo had a profound impact on Europe as soon as it appeared. It opened up the eyes of Europeans to the rich and powerful lands of the East. It inspired many explorers down the centuries. When China closed her borders to foreigners, Marco Polo's book was one of the main sources of information for Europeans about that hidden part of the world. Today, the Silk Road that Marco took has once again become a major highway across Asia, and accounts of his journeys still inspire travellers to set off on explorations, and tell others what they have seen.

A 19th-century portrait of Marco Polo as an old man, copied from a painting of 1600. It is believed to give an accurate likeness of the great traveller.

In Marco's words:

'... no other man, Christian or Saracen, Tartar or pagan, has explored so much of the world as Messer Marco, son of Messer Niccolo Polo, great and noble citizen of the city of Venice'.

(Taken from *The Travels of Marco Polo*)

Map of the Polos' travels

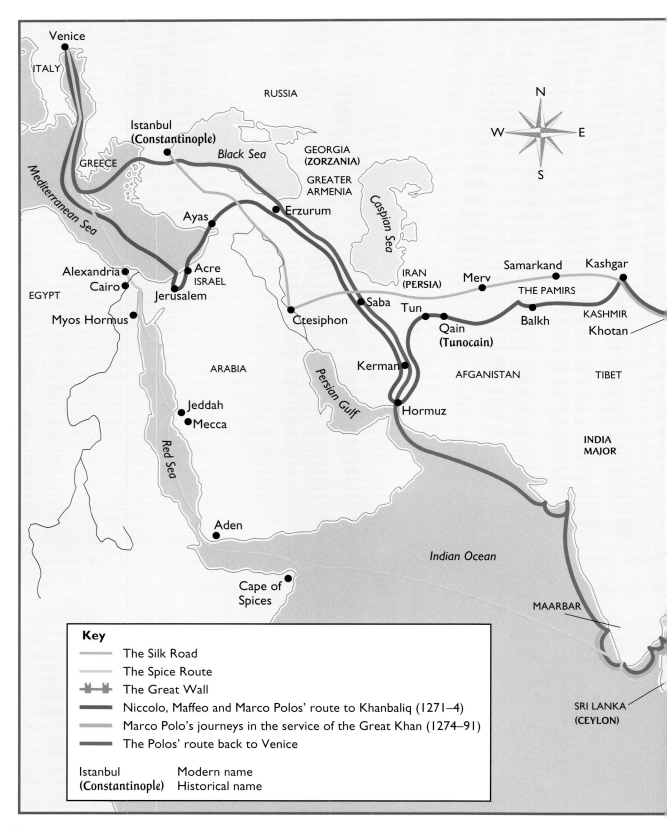

Venice
ITALY

RUSSIA

Istanbul
(Constantinople)

Black Sea

GEORGIA
(ZORZANIA)

GREATER
ARMENIA

Caspian Sea

GREECE

Mediterranean Sea

Ayas

Erzurum

Samarkand   Kashgar

Merv

THE PAMIRS

Alexandria   Acre
Cairo   ISRAEL
EGYPT   Jerusalem

IRAN
(PERSIA)

Saba
Tun

KASHMIR
Khotan

Myos Hormus

Ctesiphon

Qain
(Tunocain)

Balkh

ARABIA

Persian Gulf

Kerman

AFGANISTAN

TIBET

Jeddah
Mecca

Hormuz

INDIA
MAJOR

Red Sea

Aden

Indian Ocean

Cape of
Spices

MAARBAR

Key

▬▬	The Silk Road
▬▬	The Spice Route
▬▬	The Great Wall
▬▬	Niccolo, Maffeo and Marco Polos' route to Khanbaliq (1271–4)
▬▬	Marco Polo's journeys in the service of the Great Khan (1274–91)
▬▬	The Polos' route back to Venice

Istanbul   Modern name
(Constantinople)   Historical name

SRI LANKA
(CEYLON)

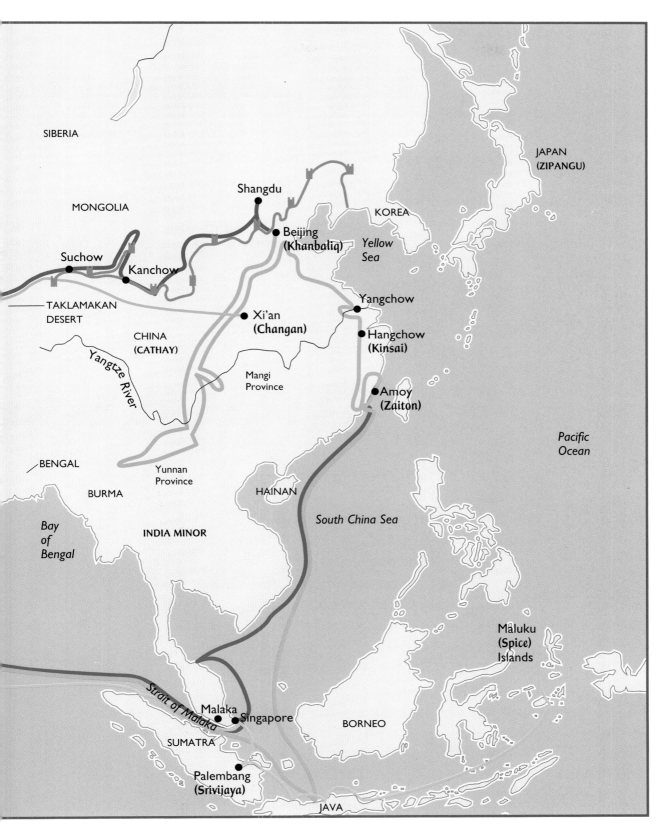

SIBERIA

MONGOLIA

Shangdu

Suchow

Kanchow

Beijing
(Khanbaliq)

KOREA

Yellow
Sea

JAPAN
(ZIPANGU)

TAKLAMAKAN
DESERT

CHINA
(CATHAY)

Yangtze River

Xi'an
(Changan)

Yangchow

Hangchow
(Kinsai)

Mangi
Province

Amoy
(Zaiton)

Pacific
Ocean

BENGAL

BURMA

Yunnan
Province

HAINAN

South China Sea

Bay
of
Bengal

INDIA MINOR

Māluku
(Spice)
Islands

Strait of Malaka

Malaka

Singapore

BORNEO

SUMATRA

Palembang
(Srivijaya)

JAVA

Timeline

1162	Birth of Genghis Khan, ruler of the Mongols.
1206	Genghis Khan unites Mongols and begins conquest of Asia.
1211	Mongols invade China.
1215	Genghis Khan captures Chung-tu (Beijing), capital of the Chinese Chin empire.
1221	Mongols attack Delhi, India.
1227	Death of Genghis Khan. His son Ogadai is elected Great Khan.
1228–9	Sixth Crusade.
1234	Mongols overthrow Chin dynasty in China.
1240	Mongols capture Kiev, Russia.
1241	Death of Ogadai Khan saves Europe from conquest by Mongols.
1246	Franciscan priest Giovanni da Pian del Carpini reaches Mongol capital at Karakorum.
1248–54	Seventh Crusade.
1250	Mameluke dynasty seizes power in Egypt.
1253	Franciscan priest William of Rubrouk reaches Karakorum.
1254	Birth of Marco Polo.
1258	Baghdad destroyed by Mongols.
1260	Kublai Khan proclaimed Great Khan.
1261	Battle of Ain Jalut in Palestine: Mongol advance halted by the Egyptians.
1265	Niccolo and Maffeo Polo first reach the Chinese capital at Khanbaliq (Beijing).
1269	Niccolo and Maffeo return to Venice.
1271	Niccolo, Maffeo and Marco Polo leave Venice for China.
1274	The three Polos reach China.
1275–92	Marco's travels in the service of Kublai Khan.
1292	The Polos leave China for home.
1294	Death of Kublai Khan.
1295	The Polos arrive back in Venice.
c.1297	Marco Polo captured and imprisoned in Genoa.
1324	Death of Marco Polo.
1325	Ibn Battuta travels from Morocco to Arabia, and eventually reaches China.
1368	The Mongols are driven out of China.
1405–33	Voyages of Cheng Ho, who may have rounded the southern tip of Africa.

| 1477 | First printed copies of *The Travels of Marco Polo* produced. |
| 1492–1504 | Inspired by *The Travels of Marco Polo*, Christopher Columbus travels westwards from Spain and discovers the Americas. |

Places to visit and further reading

Places to visit
The British Museum, London, England (fine arts of the Near and Far East)
Natural History Museum, London, England (plants and animals of the Far East)
The Louvre Museum, Paris, France (fine arts of the Near and Far East)
Peabody Museum of Archaeology and Ethnology, Cambridge, Mass., USA (peoples of the world)
Asia Society Galleries, New York, USA (fine arts of Asia)
Metropolitan Museum of Art, New York, USA (fine arts of the Near and Far East)

Websites
The Royal Geographical Society:
www.rgs.org
The History Channel:
www.thehistorychannel.co.uk/index.htm
The Silk Road:
www.silk-road.com
Discovery:
www.discovery.com

Further reading
Chrisp, Peter: *The Search for the East* (Wayland Publishers, Hove, 1993)
Humble, Richard: *The Travels of Marco Polo* (Franklin Watts, London, 1990)
Ryan, Peter: *Explorers and Mapmakers* (Evans Brothers Ltd, London, 1989)

Glossary

ambassador official who is sent abroad as a representative of a country or its ruler

artisan someone skilled at a particular job or craft

asbestos mineral made up of very fine fibres that are resistant to fire

bandit robber or member of an armed gang

banquet great feast

Buddha the title of Gautama Siddhartha (?563–483 BC). He was a religious leader born in northern India.

Buddhist someone who follows the teachings of Buddha. These state that by destroying greed and hatred, the cause of all human suffering, people can achieve perfect enlightenment.

caravan group of traders or other travellers journeying together with animals

Cathay old European name for China

Crusader follower of the military expeditions of the 11th, 12th and 13th centuries, in which the Christian powers of Europe tried to capture the Holy Land from the Muslims

dialect form of language spoken in a particular region or by a particular group of people

diplomat official, such as an ambassador, who negotiates between states or people

felt matted material made from wool or hair, made by pressing the fibres together

Franciscan member of a Christian order of monks or nuns, founded by Saint Francis of Assisi (?1181–1226)

Great Khan title of the most senior khan (ruler) in the Mongol Empire

herdsman someone who breeds and looks after cattle

Hindu follower of Hinduism, the main religion of India

illuminated decorated and coloured, often in gold

incense substance that is burnt for its pleasant-smelling, spicy smoke

junk Chinese ship, made of wood and with very high sides, flat bottom and square sails

mariner someone who travels the sea, who is skilled in navigation

merchant person who trades with other people to make a profit

Mesopotamia area in south-west Asia between the Tigris and Euphrates rivers. The word comes from the Ancient Greek, meaning 'the land between rivers'.

mirage image of an object or sheet of water caused by hot air above the ground

Mongol another (later) name for a Tartar, a person from Mongolia

musk deer type of small mountain deer from central Asia, which gives off a strong-smelling scent known as musk

navigation art of finding the right direction when making a journey

nomadic describes a member of a group of people or tribe who moves from place to place in search of food and water

pagan someone who follows any religion other than Christianity, Islam or Judaism

pageant elaborate ceremony or display

Persia present-day Iran

pope bishop of Rome and head of the Roman Catholic Church

relic something treasured because of a legend that is associated with it

sago starchy cereal used in cooking, made from the pith of the sago palm tree

Saracen Muslim

scholar learned person

Tartar old name for a person from Mongolia

yak ox (cow) of Tibet with long, shaggy hair

zebu ox with a humped back and long horns. In India and East Asia it is used as a draught animal to pull heavy loads.

Index